ARDITH HOOTEN has been writing curriculum for Scripture Press Publications for eight years, since 1973 as editor of high school curriculum. She has a wide range of experience in teaching, teacher-training, and directing Sunday School and Vacation Bible School programs and workshops. She has a B.A. from Taylor University and an M.A. in Christian education from Wheaton College.

PAUL HEIDEBRECHT is editor of **Brigade Leader,** Christian Service Brigade's magazine for men who work with teenage boys. He develops leadership training for men and coordinates adult education for Christian Service Brigade. He has a B.A. from the University of Winnipeg and an M.A. in Christian education from Wheaton College. He is an elder and is Chairman of the Christian Education Committee at Bethel Presbyterian Church, Wheaton, Ill.

Teaching Today's Teens

Relating Successfully
to High Schoolers

by Ardith Hooten
and Paul Heidebrecht

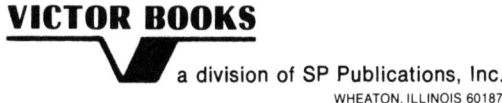

a division of SP Publications, Inc.
WHEATON, ILLINOIS 60187

Scripture quotations are from *The New International Version: New Testament* (NIV) © 1973, The New York Bible Society International. Used by permission.

ISBN: 0-88207-177-7

© 1976 by SP Publications, Inc. World rights reserved
Printed in the United States of America

VICTOR BOOKS
A division of SP Publications, Inc.
P. O. Box 1825 • Wheaton, Ill. 60187

Contents

Preface **6**

Introduction **7**

1 "I Don't Feel Adequate to Teach" **9**
2 "I Don't Feel Comfortable with Teens" **18**
3 "I Can't Get Them to Take Part" **26**
4 "I'm Not Creative Enough" **34**
5 "I'm Teaching a 'Mixed' Class" **41**

Resource Materials **46**

Preface

Basically, this book is addressed to persons whose main ministry with young people is teaching the Bible. But the focuses on building relationships and communicating God's Word through shared life experiences apply to all youth workers and parents of teens. (Check page 47 for resources on how all those ministering to teens in a church can work together to develop an effective total youth ministry.)

In writing this book, we interviewed many teachers of youth Bible study groups. Their common needs gave us direction in developing the various chapters. Their insights and victories, coupled with our own experiences, have produced some practical suggestions for overcoming many of the problems and frustrations that often accompany a ministry to teens.

Though this is not a book about team teaching, many illustrations are based on the experiences of a young couple who live in the Midwest but do not wish to be identified. We will call them Frank and Helen Linquist. These two teachers are a great inspiration—not only to their students, but to other teachers as well.

We are grateful to the teachers and young people in our lives who have challenged us, stretched our resources, and grown with us as Christians. But most of all, we are thankful to God for His Word, His Son, and His Holy Spirit who constantly probe, teach, discipline, and direct our lives.

We pray that the Holy Spirit will use this book as He works in your life—transforming you and giving you an effective ministry with teens.

Ardith Hooten
Paul Heidebrecht

Introduction

"Well, since you're in a pinch, we'll try teaching that high school group—but only for two or three months. You'd better keep looking for someone else to take over after that."

Frank and Helen Linquist still smile when they recall their answer to a desperate plea. That was four years ago, and they're still teaching!

During those years the Linquists have struggled with feelings of inadequacy, problems in relating to their students, and difficulties in getting student participation. They have learned the importance of using the right methods, and knowing what to do when interest, ages, and spiritual growth within a group vary greatly. So why are they still teaching? Because they've made some important discoveries that help them overcome the frustrations and discouragements that often plague teachers of youth. They aren't experts, but the Linquists are mastering some teaching skills that give them confidence. The "fear and trembling" they experienced when they first started teaching is gone because they've learned how to develop good relationships with their students. Most of all, they've learned how to cooperate with the Holy Spirit in the teaching-learning process.

Whether you team teach a high school group or go it alone, the insights gained by Frank and Helen can help and inspire you too.

1
"I Don't Feel Adequate to Teach"

One word can describe how Frank felt when he began teaching high schoolers four years ago—*inadequate!*

I just can't do it, Frank thought at the time. *I don't have what it takes.*

Focus on God
Many people feel inadequate to teach teens. Perhaps you do too—especially if you don't measure up to your idea of a "successful" youth worker. That was Frank's problem. To be effective, he thought he had to be athletic, have an outgoing personality, possess that special charisma that draws teens like a magnet, and have an answer for every question teens can ask.

Such characteristics may help, but they're by no means necessary. Sometimes they even get in the way. Why? Because the real key to a fruitful ministry is not in your personality or flashy programs, but in how well you communicate a Person —Jesus Christ. Assuming that you really know Christ as

Saviour and Lord, are you directing your teens' attention toward Him instead of toward yourself?

When you focus your ministry on God, something special happens. Your own inadequacies (or adequacies) fade into the background, and God begins to mold you into a person through whom He can reveal Himself to others.

When Frank realized his problem, he stopped trying to be someone he wasn't. Instead he began affirming, developing, and using the gifts God gave him and refused to let "imperfections" he couldn't change divert his attention. He accepted himself and started being a person with teens.

Be Yourself

Being a person with teens means being yourself. Just the way God is *re*creating you, making you into the image of His Son, Jesus—knocking off the rough edges and polishing you to reflect *His* personality.

In effect, you can tell your class, "Here I am; take me for what I am and for what I'm becoming. Let's explore the Scriptures together and discover what God is saying to us at this point in history. We need each other."

Being yourself means rejecting all images of a razzle-dazzle youth ministry and concentrating on God. It means getting involved with your young people in the process of learning and applying God's Word to your lives.

Reveal Yourself

Being yourself involves several closely related qualities:

Honesty One question that haunted Frank as he prepared to teach four years ago was, "What if they ask me something I don't know?" Eventually Frank realized that his students didn't expect him to be a walking Bible dictionary. So when they threw a tough question at him, he learned to say, "I don't know. But let's try to discover the answer together."

Teenagers respect honesty. And answers to difficult questions have a greater impact on their lives when *they* get involved in the research.

Transparency This second quality, similar to honesty, makes a person "knowable." A person who lacks transparency hides his real thoughts and feelings from other people. Frank recognized this problem in his life and began to do something about it.

"I was always afraid to show any emotions or reveal any weaknesses," Frank admits. "I guess I thought it would threaten my masculinity or my position as a teacher. When I finally saw the stifling effect this had on my relationships with others, I really worked at coming out of my shell. One day I admitted to my students that I worry a lot about the future and what the world will be like when my three small children are grown. The response of the students was remarkable. Most of them empathized. And for the first time, several young people ventured to share some of *their* real fears too. By looking into God's Word, we were able to work through these fears together.

"This new openness added a dimension to our group that wasn't there before. As the weeks passed, we developed a genuine concern for one another that produced more openness and spiritual growth as well."

Frank and his students experienced something that can happen in most interpersonal relationships: The more you reveal of your inner self (become transparent), the more others will reveal themselves to you.

This doesn't mean you should display false modesty, put yourself down, or tell your teens everything you've ever thought or done. It simply means letting them see you as a human being who understands *their* humanity. So in addition to communicating Bible knowledge, be sure to share your personal feelings, emotions, values, and decisions with your students. This can enable you to minister to teens as *whole* persons because they will see you as a whole person.

Trust Closely tied to transparency, trust involves depending on another person or group of persons for reliable friendship. When you trust someone, you respect his or her ideas, personality traits, and background. Like transparency, trust is usually returned by a person who receives it.

Frank learned to respect the teenagers in his Bible study group. He began caring about their opinions and feelings. He developed a real interest in their school activities, hobbies, and family relationships. In return, the teens began to respect and trust Frank. They grew to respect him not only as a teacher, but as a person—a friend.

Be Transformed

Being yourself is a starting point in teaching teens, but it's not enough. Qualities of honesty, transparency, and trust cannot come by an act of sheer willpower. To a certain degree, they can be learned, but they need an outside Source of power and influence—the Holy Spirit. He recreates us—sinful, selfish people that we are—into persons who can relate to other people (including teenagers) with honesty, transparency, and trust.

The Bible describes this process of recreation beautifully in the well-known list of Spirit-produced fruit (Gal. 5:22-23). Seeing how God is developing these qualities in his own life helps Frank feel comfortable about teaching and challenging his students to grow spiritually too.

Love—not a mushy sentimentality or even an unending desire to be with teenagers—expresses itself in genuine concern for teens just as they are and for their potentials as Christian adults.

At first, Frank found it hard to love some of the teens in his class. But as he prayed for each one individually, God increased his capacity to love. Soon his prayers became spontaneous and more frequent, and his interest in each student grew more genuine.

Joy—not a life-of-the-party exuberance—is a deep satisfaction in knowing Christ personally and growing spiritually.

In spite of Frank's quiet manner, his joy in Christ really comes through to the students he teaches. They're definitely attracted to it.

Peace is a sense of contentment that comes from total dependence on God.

Frank is learning what this peace means. That's why he can risk being transparent with his students.

Patience—not just tolerance—is a real understanding of individual needs and a willingness to wait on God to do *His* work of perfecting each teen in *His* own time.

Frank had little patience when he first started teaching. He got upset because the young people didn't always act as mature adults. But gradually he realized that teens are *not* mature adults—they're people in transition who need love, understanding, and patient guidance.

Goodness is a commitment to what is right—to what is clearly stated in Scripture as God's will.

Frank's own commitment to God's Word is quite visible to his students. He hates injustice and evil. At the same time, he admits his weaknesses and shares how God is helping him grow. Through the testimony of Frank's life, many teens have been persuaded to live for Christ too.

Faithfulness means dependability, reliability; a hard thing to learn but it's absolutely necessary.

Frank has always been a man of his word. But he's learned that failing to keep even little promises can mean losing teens' trust and respect. So he thinks things through before making promises, and keeps the promises he makes.

Gentleness means sensitivity to each teen's feelings, making sure his or her ideas are accepted and respected, watching for signs of hurt or pain that accompany adolescent years.

Frank knows that being a good Bible teacher—one who rightly handles the Word of God—means being a person God is changing and developing. He has to be the "real thing" in whom teens can see God's work going on.

Committed teachers of the Bible usually recognize their inadequacies. They realize how small their Bible knowledge is compared with the infinite depth of God's Holy Word. They struggle with wrong attitudes and motivations that can spoil human relationships.

But that doesn't stop them from teaching. It only makes them depend more on God, and that's good! The fact that the Holy Spirit is working in them and through them as persons is their source of encouragement.

The Apostle Paul recognized the same thing about himself when he wrote to the Corinthian Christians. Paul said, "When I came to you, brothers, I did not come with eloquence or superior wisdom as I proclaimed to you the testimony about God" (1 Cor. 2:1). Paul frankly admitted, "I came to you in weakness and fear, and with much trembling" (2:3). But then he stated, "My message and my preaching were not with wise and persuasive words, but with a demonstration of the Spirit's power so that your faith might not rest on men's wisdom, but on God's power" (2:4-5).

Be Empowered

The effectiveness of Paul's preaching is attributed to the power of the Holy Spirit. And there are several reasons why the Holy Spirit is important in your teaching ministry:

He is the Author of Truth. About the Gospel message, Paul said, "We speak of God's secret wisdom, a wisdom that has been hidden and that God destined for our glory before time began" (2:7). "But," Paul added, "God has revealed it [this wisdom] to us by His Spirit" (2:10). We now have that wisdom in written form—the Bible. The Holy Spirit is its Author.

He interprets the Truth. "We have not received the spirit of the world, but the Spirit who is from God, that we may understand what God has freely given us" (2:12). The truth of the Bible has to be "spiritually discerned" (2:14), and for this we need the Holy Spirit. He is absolutely essential to the process of our learning and responding to the Word of God.

He declares Truth and uses it to instruct, remind, and guide believers. Near the end of His earthly ministry, Jesus talked a lot about the Holy Spirit, giving more insights into the Spirit's role. Jesus told His disciples, "The Holy Spirit, whom the Father will send in My name, will teach you all things and will remind you of everything I have said to you" (John 14:26). "He will guide you into all truth . . . and He will tell you what is yet to come" (16:13). Though Jesus' words applied primarily to the disciples who later wrote much of the New Testament, they also apply to Christians today.

Be Used

Where does that leave you as a teacher of God's Word? Simply as an instrument of the Holy Spirit. You can't change the attitudes or actions of a teenager or produce spiritual growth. You can't even make the Bible come alive in the heart and mind of a young person. Only the Holy Spirit can cause these changes. But He chooses to work through Christians who are willing to be partners with Him in the process.

You can work with the Holy Spirit several ways to reach teens for Christ:

Be living proof of what the Bible teaches. A teenager's image of what God can do in a person's life may depend on what he sees God doing in *your* life. The reality and relevance of the Bible to a teen's life may depend on how he sees the Bible fitting into *your* life. His opinion of Jesus Christ may depend on you because you claim to be Christ's disciple.

So your role is one of a model. This doesn't mean you have to be a perfect example of Jesus Christ—that's impossible. But you can be a model of a committed disciple, reflecting the image of Christ as you are being transformed into His likeness.

Remember, even if you are not the only or primary model in your students' lives, you are still an important influence as they grow toward maturity.

Be a facilitator of biblical learning. If the Holy Spirit really does the teaching, then your job is to arrange circumstances so He can teach effectively. This includes guiding teens in discovering biblical truth and helping them apply it to their lives. By getting teens "into" the Word, you set the stage for the Holy Spirit to do His work.

Be a supportive member of a community of believers. Christians don't grow in a vacuum. God did not design spiritual growth that way. Rather, He created a community of believers called the church which exists for the spiritual growth of all its members. Each member in his daily work for Christ should support and encourage the others. Though your young people may not yet be integrated into the total body life of the church, they can learn the basics of what it means to be a community of believers by participating in a Bible study group where mutual support and encouragement exist. The Holy Spirit ministers to a class member through other students and the teacher. But He also ministers to the teacher through students!

Be courageous in the Spirit. How can the Holy Spirit's involvement in the teaching-learning process relieve any feelings of inadequacy you may have? It helped Frank by giving him a whole new picture of his role as a Bible teacher. The divine perspective of the Holy Spirit as the real Teacher gave Frank hope and vision. It also gave him courage because he could see that the ultimate success of teaching did not depend on him alone, but on the power of the Holy Spirit.

Ask Yourself

In what ways is my ministry focused on myself? On God?

In what areas do I still need to be myself and reveal myself to my class?

How can I be a more effective partner of the Holy Spirit in our ministry to teens?

Do Yourself

Jot down the list of Spirit-produced fruit discussed in this chapter. Beside each fruit, indicate what evidence you have seen of it in your own life in recent months. Ask the Holy Spirit to reveal and cleanse you of any wrong attitudes or motives that might hinder the growth of His fruit in your life and in the lives of your students. (Note: *The Penetrators*, by Pat Hurley gives additional help in developing yourself as an effective youth worker. See Resource Materials, page 47.)

Prayer for Adequacy

Dear Lord, in and of myself, I am inadequate to teach teens. But I know your Holy Spirit is more than adequate and more than willing to teach teens through me. Help me be myself. Transform me, empower me, and use me for *Your* glory and not my own. Amen.

2
"I Don't Feel Comfortable with Teens"

Helen hesitated when she and Frank were asked to teach. She liked teens, but she felt intimidated by them.

Can I identify with them? she wondered. *After all, I'm over 30. Even my 23-year-old sister says she sometimes feels "out of it" around teenagers.*

Rapid Culture Change
Helen's feelings of uneasiness are understandable. Youth today live in a world that's different from what it was 20, 15, or even 10 years ago. They face pressures unknown to previous generations.

For example, young people of Helen's generation—the late '50s—faced an optimistic future. Education held promises of good jobs, prosperity, and a meaningful life, despite the Cold War threats of nuclear catastrophe. Like many of her peers, Helen applied herself to her schoolwork, honestly believing that an educated person would be a more fulfilled person.

Youth today don't face such an optimistic future. College degrees don't deliver the jobs they used to. The potential threats of worldwide food and energy shortages and overpopulation are frightening. The breaking up of the family unit and transient life-styles of many families shake young people's security. Various liberation movements cause additional problems with personal identity. It's no wonder many young people, confused and disillusioned, battle constantly with recurrent despair, or eventually give in to it.

This mood is quite different from that of the '60s when young people were caught up in an antiestablishment idealism that sent them into the streets with slogans and banners. "Student power" eventually fizzled and a new generation of young people has now emerged.

These examples simply show that the world of youth is undergoing constant culture changes. What was true last year won't necessarily be true next year. Cultural gaps do exist and keeping up with them isn't always easy. But there are some things you can do to try: (1) Subscribe to periodicals such as *Youthletter* and *Success With Youth Report* (see Resource Materials, page 47). (2) Visit local high schools. Check the required subjects and reading lists. Examine magazines and books available to teens in the school library. (3) Talk with schoolteachers and teens about values, expectations, and cultural trends peculiar to your own locality. (4) Subscribe to religious and nonreligious magazines that appeal to teens. (5) Listen to music that's popular among teens.

Peer influence is particularly strong among teens. Because all young people (including Christians) absorb some attitudes and values of their culture, it's important to know what those attitudes and values are. For example, the current trend in teen culture may be to think of *commitment* as only a temporary thing: "I'm committed to you today—heart, soul, and spirit. But that doesn't mean I'll be committed to you next year, next month, or even next week." If this definition of commitment gets through to one of your students, how will it affect his concept of what you mean when you challenge him to commit his life to Christ? (For deeper insights into the worldly philosophies that can influence your youth, read *The Magic Bubble*—see Resource Material, page 46.)

No Easy Labels

Though greatly influenced by his peers, each young person is a unique individual. He can't be described simply in a generalized way, according to the youth culture.

When Helen discovered this, her attitude really changed. She no longer views teens as "rebellious," "apathetic," or "disrespectful." She has discovered that each one is a real live person who's struggling to cope with a pressure-filled world and trying to progress toward some vaguely defined goals. Helen considers each teen in the context of his family, still a great influence on his life. And she recognizes that most teens pass through periods of spiritual dryness and spiritual fervor—seeming to reach maturity but never quite getting there.

Gradually Helen's feelings of intimidation subsided. She still feels the cultural gap sometimes, but she finds she can almost always identify with her students' basic problems. They ask many of the same questions she asked as a teen. They worry about many of the same things: personal identity and relationships with friends, family, and the opposite sex. They wonder about the future and search for life's meaning.

Helen can also relate to their emotions. When they feel lonely, discouraged, fearful, or joyful she understands. She's been there too. And because emotions are timeless, Helen can point teens to Scripture for the comfort, encouragement, peace, and real joy experienced by real people who lived thousands of years ago.

Helen states, "The teen years are very emotional. The kids are wondering about the future, but mostly they're concerned about who they are as people. They feel a real push and pull between their relationships with their parents and friends. Though they want to cut themselves loose from the 'apron strings,' they still need some security from those ties. I'm not sure how much of this is cultural and how much is a natural characteristic of adolescents. In any case, it seems to be a necessary part of the growing-up process. Realizing this has helped me relate more comfortably to teens."

Bridging the Gaps

An increased understanding of teenagers helped Helen discern some very practical ways to relate to them—which was exactly what she thought she couldn't do. If you have problems relating to your teens, perhaps some of the following guidelines can help you too:

Be patient. Teens don't always act like mature adults because they're not. If you learn to be patient with fluctuating moods and behavior, it will pay off in closer relationships and fruitful class discussions. On the other hand, teens are capable of adult behavior, so treat them accordingly. Talking down to them is definitely out. So are assignments and activities that are just "busywork."

Listen actively. When talking with someone, do you ever find yourself just waiting for him to stop talking so you can speak? That's *passive* listening. *Active* listening means caring enough about another person to give him your full attention. Because you want to learn more about him, your responses are usually questions designed to keep *him* talking. In a group setting, you are sensitive to each person and how much the group is listening to the person who is speaking. And you try to draw each person's ideas out, encouraging him to share.

Relate as a friend. Establishing a friendship with a teenager is much like establishing a friendship with anyone else. It means getting acquainted with each other's backgrounds, interests, and concerns; having spontaneous get-togethers; and reinforcing each other in positive ways.

A friendship progresses to personal experiences together, shared memories of these experiences, and a sense of loyalty to each other. All these ingredients can be developed in your relationships with teens.

Guide by example. A teacher who expects teens to do what he says simply because he's boss, has a hard time developing close relationships. Some teens may outwardly obey such negative authority, but they rarely respect it.

As a teacher you *are* an authority figure, but your authority should be positive, not negative. How? *First,* earn your teens' respect, and they will willingly accept your authority. Earning respect comes from practicing what you preach, being a friend, and being genuine and honest.

Second, rest your authority on God and His Word. If you submit yourself and your teaching to the authority of God's Word, you will direct teens' attention away from yourself to God. And that's the beginning of true Christian living. This does not mean using the Bible as a club to get teens in line. Rather, it involves motivating and guiding teens by example, more than by word, to obey God's Word *independently* of any human authority—including yours.

Reaping the Harvest

Frank and Helen have taught teens for four years now and can see growth in their students' relationships with them and with God.

Students and teachers   Helen happily reports, "Some of the young people who were in our Bible study groups—especially those who were with us for three or four years—

have become our close friends. Some who are away at school still write to us and stop by to see us when they're in town." Such relationships took several years to build. In hindsight, Helen can't see how they could have developed in any less time. But the time spent was worth it because relationships like these usually prove to be deep and lasting.

Probably it isn't possible to have a close relationship with every teen in your class, but it's a goal to work toward. Perhaps you get frustrated because you think you should spend hours every week getting together with your students as individuals and as a group. This might be ideal, but it's not always practical. Remember, the quality of the time you spend with your students is often more important than the quantity. If you can communicate with teens as *whole* persons during the study hour, even those young people on the fringes will likely be drawn to you for friendship or guidance. Sensitivity to the Holy Spirit and to students' responses can alert you to times when you should give individual students special attention outside of your regularly scheduled Bible study.

Students and God Spiritual growth will always be a source of wonder for those who teach the Bible. Though the New Testament is filled with indicators of spiritual growth, it's extremely difficult to pin down specific criteria to measure spiritual growth in anyone.

The Apostle Paul provided a set of indicators (Col. 1:9-11) called the "Colossian Cycle" by Larry Richards in *Creative Bible Teaching*. The indicators include knowing biblical truth ("a knowledge of His will"), understanding it as it applies to one's personal life ("spiritual wisdom and understanding"), actually responding to the truth with action ("living a life worthy of the Lord"), ("serving God with results, bearing fruit in every good work"), and knowing God better ("growing in the knowledge of God").

At least two principles are suggested by these indicators.

First, knowing God personally is different from knowing about God. Both are absolutely necessary. Unfortunately, many students only know about God. Effective teaching helps teens meet God personally as well as intellectually.

Second, all Bible teaching should lead to personal response by the student. It's not enough to learn information or even what the Bible says about a given topic. Teens, like adults, must personally apply the truth they learn to their own lives. They must obey what God tells them to do.

Programming for Process

"We were excited when we began to see evidences of spiritual growth in some of our students," Helen says. "For that we thanked God. We knew it was the work of the Holy Spirit. But we wondered about the others in the group. Many had shown little or no spiritual growth—at least none we could detect. They just drifted along, not really coming to grips with the reality of Christ in their lives. Had we failed? We wondered."

Spiritual growth will not always come when and how you would like to see it. But after you have done your part as a facilitator of truth, spiritual growth is up to the Holy Spirit and each person's free will. You simply cannot program the Holy Spirit or how and when others will respond to Him. And you can't program the final product either. Growth takes time. So you can only help teens move toward spiritual maturity. *Programming for process, not product, is the key to understanding spiritual growth among teens.*

Even a teen who is vitally interested in spiritual things is still a "babe in Christ" compared with his growth potential. God has begun a work in his life that will need to continue through his adult years.

Teens are in the process of making decisions that will affect the rest of their lives. They are open to the options. So it's a crucial time to face non-Christians with the claims of Christ and help Christians establish their feet firmly in their own independent faith in God before they enter college or the workaday world.

Ask Yourself

How do I feel when I'm with teenagers in my church and in my community? Do I feel uncomfortable? If so, why?

What kind of "identity struggle" did I go through as a teen?

In what ways could I build better relationships between myself and my students?

What evidences of spiritual growth do I see in the lives of my students?

Do Yourself

Write down three specific things you plan to do this week to help you learn more about current teen culture.

Write down the names of two "problem" teens in your class. Determine ways in which you can get to know them better, learn their real needs, and lead them to Christ and/or encourage their spiritual growth.

Prayer for Courage

Lord, some of the teenagers I know intimidate me. I don't understand them. Help me build relationships with them. Give me patience to listen actively. Use me to help them grow spiritually—by the grace and power of Your Holy Spirit. Amen.

3
"I Can't Get Them to Take Part"

Frank and Helen have vivid memories of their first few weeks of teaching.

"We started with seven girls and four boys," Frank reports. "We gritted our teeth and prepared for the worst. We didn't know any of the teens very well, but we expected to be 'walked all over.' We knew at least two youth sponsors had quit in frustration with the same group. But to our surprise, the teens didn't walk all over us. Obviously bored, they just sat there."

After recovering from the shock, Frank and Helen began asking themselves some hard questions. "What tuned them out? Was it our lesson plan? The way we taught? How can we excite teens to take part in meaningful Bible study and group discussions?"

From various sources Helen and Frank discovered several basic facts they needed to consider in motivating teens to participate in the teaching-learning process.

Consider the Teens

One set of motivational factors involves how a lesson's approach and content meet the needs of the students.

Is it relevant to their needs? No one, including adults, is very interested in learning about something that has little to do with his major interests. For example, if a salesman comes to your door, you soon determine your response to him on the basis of whether his product is of any value to you. If it's irrelevant to your needs, you don't buy it (unless the salesman is most persuasive). The same applies to conferences you attend, adult electives you choose, activities in which you become involved, and countless other opportunities.

Teens approach Sunday School classes and other Bible study groups on the same basis. Whether a study topic is doctrinal or problematic, it's unlikely to interest teens if it isn't related to their needs or is approached in an academic, abstract, or impersonal way. But if teens can see how a topic touches or relates to their real needs or experiences, motivation can be triggered. Like a salesman, a teacher must sometimes link a student's need with the product (content) by giving an illustration, demonstration, or case study.

How can you discover the needs that trigger teen interest? By getting to know the teens personally. Some needs are experienced by almost all teens. These include getting along with family members, choosing friends, learning to be responsible, feeling good about themselves (self-image), developing healthy relationships with members of the opposite sex, and establishing an inner value system. For Christian teens, all these needs should be met through Scripture and their personal relationships with God.

As you get to know your students better, you can move from general needs to the specific needs of each student. For example, Henry's weight problem is caused by a negative self-image. The class probably won't discuss Henry's weight, but if the lesson touches Henry's real need (self-acceptance), he can be helped to apply what he learns to his own situation. Once Henry believes that God loves him as a unique individual, he can be led to return God's love, accept himself, and take personal responsibility for the proper care of his body.

All youth workers in a church should get together to plan a strategy for their church's total youth ministry. And choosing and correlating Bible content to be studied in Sunday School and during the week is one of their major tasks. (For help in evaluating and shaping your church's total youth ministry, use *Where's It At?*—see Resource Materials, page 47.)

A balanced teen curriculum includes Bible surveys, books, biographies, core passages, topics, apologetics, and biblical perspectives on current issues.

Dated Bible curriculum is usually carefully designed to make sure teens receive a balanced diet of life-related Bible study during their years in the youth department. Elective courses, while popular with youth, must be carefully controlled by the church staff to make certain a balanced diet is received. Ideally, both dated and elective materials can be used by a church. Both can be offered in separate classes on Sunday morning; or one can be used for Sunday School while the other is used for group Bible study during the week. But the material chosen for any particular group should "scratch students where they itch" or sometimes where they *should* itch! If your group is basically made up of Christian young people who are eager or easily motivated to grow spiritually (a core group), the material you choose will probably be different from material you'd choose to use with a group consisting mostly of apathetic Christians or non-Christians (a fringe group). So it's important for you to know your students and their special needs.

Can they get personally involved in it? Few people respond to truth on a purely intellectual level. Feelings and wills usually get involved and, in most cases, have more to do with motivation than people's intellects.

For example, recall a disagreement you've had with another person. What were the objective facts on both sides? What feelings did you have about the other person? About his actions? About yourself? Were you prepared to change your behavior if you were proved wrong? Did you operate totally on an intellectual level?

Unfortunately, much teaching is aimed only at the intellect, ignoring emotion and will. This imbalance often reduces student participation. Teaching that does not involve a teen's whole being leaves out "big chunks" of his personality that need to be touched by God. But when these "chunks" are involved in the learning process, a student usually responds enthusiastically.

When the Bible is taught as pure information, the teaching is not being done as God intended. If students are allowed to express how they feel about a truth (gut response) and what they plan to do about it, participation usually increases.

Does it challenge them? Some teens are "lazy" or listless because of the great physical changes which are sapping their strength. Others appear lazy and apathetic because they haven't been challenged by something that really tests their personal abilities and characters.

Teens do respond to challenge. Witness the success of various outdoor stress camps for young people, missionary service projects sponsored by many mission boards, and community and church activities in which teens handle major responsibilities.

Your teaching should challenge teens to a disciplined dedicated life of service to Christ.

Are they free to express their views? We all enjoy close relationships in which we are free to express our opinions honestly without damaging the relationships. We want to be able to open up and still be accepted just as we are.

The Christian community is designed to be that way, and your high school class can experience it too. Teens usually respond positively if they feel accepted and trust the other members of the group, especially their teacher. Close personal relationships provide a context for free, open discussions. For many teachers this is a truly rewarding aspect of teaching.

Developing these close personal relationships takes time though. That's why good class participation may not occur during the first few weeks of teaching.

Set the Mood

The personal relationships between you, your students, and God are factors that motivate student participation.

Love each student and express your love through personal involvement in their lives. To do this, you may want to attend school functions in which your students have parts, or other outside-the-class activities. But in-class sharing and concern can also be effective.

Foster mutual acceptance in which you and your students become fellow-learners of God's Word. You can generate an atmosphere of learning by conveying a real desire to learn from the teens' insights into the Word.

Develop a group life in which members encourage one another. In a mature group, members take responsibility for one another, assume leadership, and show personal dedication to the group. A group matures as relationships are built. This requires time for *socializing* (getting to know each other as persons) as well as *studying*.

Since all members should be drawn into the life of the group, make a special effort to reach teens who sit on the sidelines or seem unaccepted by others in the group. These students need your love and acceptance. They also need to feel accepted by their peers. Your example will help students learn to accept and care about them. Teens who are slow, shy, or unattractive in some way often contribute a great deal to the whole class when they're helped to blossom spiritually and socially. This helps them become even more acceptable to their peers.

Be an example of one who lives out the truth he teaches. As a reality factor you can stifle or stimulate group life.

Hold teens accountable for responding to God's truth in obedience. Because God's Word calls for an obedient response, you can't ignore how students are actually living. Follow up on the teens in succeeding classes to see how they are practicing the truths they have learned. Praise those who are trying and gently encourage those who are lagging (on an individual basis). Self-discipline and personal responsibility should be your goals for each student in your class.

Create a sharing atmosphere through proper facilities. Your meeting place can actually hinder student participation. If it's a cold unattractive room in the church, ask permission for teens to decorate it to their own tastes so they'll feel at home in it. If your Bible study group convenes during the week, meet in the warm atmosphere of various students' homes. (This is a good way to get parents involved in the youth ministry too.) Also, sharing is easier if students sit in a circle or semicircle rather than in straight rows. When possible, sit with your students. This helps break down an invisible but often real barrier.

Depend on the Spirit

Of course, the most important factor in motivating student participation and response is a Person—the Holy Spirit.

The Holy Spirit is intimately involved in the whole process of Bible teaching precisely because the Bible is the tool the Holy Spirit uses to change people's lives. This distinguishes

Bible teaching from all other kinds of teaching. How is the Holy Spirit active in motivating us?

He creates a desire for God whom we meet in Scripture. The Apostle Paul wrote that the Spirit lives in all those who are in Christ (Rom. 8:9) and live according to the Spirit (8:4). The Spirit makes us children of God, who cry "Abba, Father" (8:15). We can have an intimate relationship with God the Father because of the Holy Spirit.

He exposes our sinful natures. Paul knew that "the sinful nature desires what is contrary to the Spirit, and the Spirit what is contrary to the sinful nature. They are in conflict with each other, so that you do not do what you want" (Gal. 5:17). This tension between the Holy Spirit and our sinful human natures will be with us as long as we are earth-bound. But we depend on Him, the Spirit helps us "put to death the misdeeds of the body" (Rom. 8:13). If we fail to repent of our sins, we grieve the Spirit (Eph. 4:30), but if we do repent, we experience the joy of forgiveness applied to us by the Spirit through Christ.

He helps us grasp the meaning of God's Word. Jesus told His disciples that the Holy Spirit would make known to them what belongs to Christ (John 16:14-15). And Jesus gave them the words God gave to Him (17:8). These words, now found in our Bible, are what the Holy Spirit makes known to us. Without the work of the Holy Spirit, the Bible is just another book for those who read it. The Holy Spirit alone can motivate readers to respond to God.

He helps apply God's Word to our lives. The Holy Spirit involves our whole personalities and makes God's Word relevant and challenging. Our conduct is now directed by Him (Rom. 8:4) who produces spiritual fruit in our lives (Gal. 5:22) and fills us (Eph. 5:18-20) so our relationships are clearly affected.

All these activities of the Holy Spirit are essential if teens are to be motivated to study God's Word. They are also essential if *you* want to learn. Recognizing the work of the Holy Spirit is the first step. Praying that the Holy Spirit will do this work in your class is the next. Giving Him the glory (even when you don't see the results) is the final step.

Frank and Helen Linquist were fairly green at motivating their high school students when they started teaching. This deficiency was part of the reason for the teens' poor response. But the Linquists learned how to consider the teens' needs, create a challenging atmosphere, aim for a goal, and depend on the Spirit. You can too.

Ask Yourself

Are the lessons I teach relevant to my teens' needs?

Can my students get personally involved with the content of the lessons?

How do the lessons challenge them to disciplined, dedicated service for Christ?

Is there freedom in my class for teens to share their views and feelings?

What evidence is in my life of the Holy Spirit's motivating me?

Do Yourself

Evaluate the last class you taught according to the various motivational factors described in this chapter. Make specific plans to work on those factors which seem to be missing from your teaching-learning process.

Prayer for Motivation

Lord, the teens in my class are in Your hands. Only You can really motivate them. Help me not to get in Your way. Help me to build relationships with the students and make my class an exciting place to learn. Amen.

4
"I'm Not Creative Enough"

Frank and Helen hadn't finished their first year of teaching when they attended an all day teacher-training seminar to get new ideas for sparking student interest. They were exposed to so many creative teaching methods that they hardly knew which ones to start using first.

The Big Show
The Linquists' class took on a new look after the seminar—like the green leaves of summer turning into a host of colors. Sometimes the teens were hard-pressed to keep up. But attendance became more consistent as "fringe" teens came out to see the "big show."

Then interest dropped off. The teens became noticeably restless and dissatisfied. Frank couldn't understand it at first. Finally he and Helen asked the class for an honest evaluation of the past few months. The teens had difficulty explaining their dissatisfaction. Then Joanne hit the nail on the head: "All these things we're doing are fun, but I don't think we're learning much!"

The Linquists were disillusioned. They knew that methods which foster student participation are educationally and biblically sound. Learners who take part actively in the teaching-learning process learn up to 80 percent more than passive learners who merely sit and listen. Jesus used many different kinds of teaching methods throughout His ministry, including case studies, questions, illustrations, parables, object lessons, personal examples, and student assignments.

"There's nothing wrong with the methods we've been using," Frank told Helen on their way home from church. "I think we just went overboard and used them in the wrong ways."

"Let's dust off our seminar notes," Helen suggested. "In our eagerness to be creative, maybe we missed some important aspects of the teaching-learning process that affect what methods we should use and when to use them."

Life-Response Aim

Seeing obvious weaknesses in using the lecture method alone, some teachers overreact and use all kinds of methods indiscriminately. As a result, their lessons may wander all over the place and end up nowhere. Or the methods used so "upstage" important Bible content that no one can figure out the point of the lesson. (That's what the Linquists discovered about their teaching.)

Methods are not ends in themselves; they are a means to an end. Used correctly, methods are carefully planned learning activities led by a teacher to guide each student toward a specific life response. Stated in terms of a lesson aim, the life response should be something each teacher wants to see happen in the lives of his students as a result of their personal encounters with God and His Word.

The life-response aim is usually stated in terms of behavior or action—an outward expression of an inward response to

God. For example, the life-response aim for a lesson on witnessing might be: *To guide teens in planning and taking part in a specific evangelistic outreach project.* Once a teacher has this life-response aim clearly in mind, he can begin planning how to teach the lesson.

Guided Discovery Learning
Students should not simply be *told* what the Bible says and what they ought to do about it. Real spiritual growth is more likely to take place when a teacher *guides* students in discovering and responding to Bible truths for themselves. This approach to learning, which focuses on the learners instead of the teacher, is called *guided discovery learning.*

With *guided discovery learning,* methods are chosen to help students (1) FOCUS attention on the lesson topic, (2) DISCOVER Bible truths and their practical applications for teens today, and (3) actively RESPOND to God and His Word. When methods are used for these purposes, what happens to the lesson?

The lesson has structure and direction. FOCUS, DISCOVER, and RESPOND provide the structure for building a lesson plan. And specific purposes developed for each of these three lesson parts provide direction. A teacher who knows where he's going is more likely to choose right methods.

The lesson is designed to meet learners' needs, not display teacher talents. When used correctly, methods involve a learner actively each step of the way, with the ultimate goal of helping him apply practical Bible truths to his life.

The lesson becomes a process of discovery for each learner. Instead of being told to "sit and listen," students are invited to "come and see."

This emphasis on learner participation in the *guided discovery learning* process is the secret of creative teaching. A teacher who plans his lessons accordingly makes way for the Holy Spirit to work creatively in the lives of teens, molding and making them into the image of Jesus Christ. For such a teacher, methods are tools, not gimmicks.

Lesson Plan Methods

How is a lesson planned so the emphasis is on getting learners into God's Word and helping them respond to it in personal ways? Let's establish some guidelines for choosing right methods by examining the *guided discovery learning* process in more detail.

FOCUS *Purpose: To motivate teens for Bible study by focusing teen interests and needs to be dealt with by the Bible passage.*

Some methods which might accomplish this task are role play, case study, question/answer, skit, personal testimony, thought questions, agree/disagree, and debate. For example, if the topic is *witnessing,* two students might debate: *Resolved: Every Christian is a witness.* After a brief debate, a teacher could lead naturally into the Bible study by posing questions such as: What *is* a witness? What does God say about witnessing? What are the characteristics of an effective witness?

DISCOVER *Purpose: To guide teens in discovering specific Bible truth and how it relates to their lives today.*

Once teens have been motivated for Bible study, the first step of discovery can begin. This step appeals mainly to teens' *intellects,* helping them dig out biblical facts and principles. It should be planned in terms of what a teacher wants his students to *know* as a result of Bible study. Though lecture may sometimes be appropriate, a teacher should usually choose methods that can help students study the Bible for themselves. Question/answer, Bible search (individual or group), research reports, outlining, and paraphrasing are some of the methods that can be used. *Who, what, when,* and *where* questions help students discover facts, while *why* and *how* questions help them dig out basic principles for dealing with life needs. It's important to delve deeply into the Word, not being satisfied with simplistic answers and formulas. It's equally important to study the passage in its full context, trying to understand what the author was saying to his original readers before trying to decide what the passage means for Christians today.

The process of discovery continues as students link what has been discovered in the Word with their own experience. As in FOCUS, this step in the teaching-learning process zeros in on teen interests and needs. Methods chosen should guide students in thinking about and verbalizing specific ways the Bible truth studied can make a difference in their attitudes and actions toward God, themselves, and others. Some methods effective in accomplishing this purpose are brainstorming, group discussion, life situations with questions, question/answer, research/reports, and role play. The method or methods used should lead each teen right up to the ultimate aim of the lesson—a personal life response.

RESPOND *Purpose: To help teens respond in obedience to God.* This step in the lesson plan appeals to teens' *emotions* and *wills*. A teacher plans according to what students should FEEL and/or DO in response to the Truth studied.

Knowing what to do is not the same as doing it! The transfer of Bible truth to life does not come automatically. It's seldom enough for a teacher to simply tell students, "God's Word says Christians should witness, so be sure to witness this week." Even giving a challenging illustration of someone else's witnessing experience is no guarantee that students will go right out and share the Gospel. The teacher must help each teen make a personal application of God's Word and give him an opportunity to put that application (response) into practice. Some methods that help do this are decision cards, written responses, personal evaluations, personal sharing, and personal and/or group projects. For example, in the case of a lesson on witnessing, Christian teens should be given an opportunity to actually plan and take part in individual or group outreach projects.

FOCUS, DISCOVER, and RESPOND add up to a total learning experience that is a discovery from beginning to end. The lesson begins by surfacing teens' felt and real needs. Students are then led into the Bible to discover how God's plan for the ages can meet their needs. Finally, each teen is given an opportunity to respond personally to God's Word, allowing it to change his life. A teacher plans the lesson in terms of what students should KNOW, FEEL, and DO as a result of their encounter with God and His Word.

Frank and Helen find that the lesson plans in their teacher's manual are structured according to this *guided discovery learning* process. All they have to do is adjust some of the aims and methods to meet the particular needs of their students. They don't become slaves to the curriculum, but they let the curriculum work for them. When a method suggested fits their particular needs, they use it; when it doesn't, they choose another method that will work better for them. They use methods based on the *guided discovery learning* concept, and also on their own abilities, the class area, the characteristics, needs, and abilities of their students, the class size, and the teaching time available. In any case, they plan carefully so all three steps (FOCUS, DISCOVER, RESPOND) in the teaching-learning process are included. Since every minute is valuable, they strive for *total hour teaching* so everything that happens from the moment the first student arrives till the last one leaves is directed toward achieving a specific life response to God's Word from each student.

After exploring *total hour teaching,* the Linquist's Sunday School staff dropped its weekly department assembly. It was taking up at least 15 minutes of valuable class time each week and contained nothing that related to the day's Bible lesson.

The staff found that everything being done during department assemblies (announcements, taking attendance, singing, receiving offerings, etc.) could be handled in other ways or were simply duplications of church-time or youth group experiences. They even expanded their *total hour teaching* by providing students with take-home papers which contained lesson-related articles and features.

Ask Yourself

What methods do I use in teaching my class?

Are the methods teacher-centered or pupil-centered?

How did the last lesson I taught help teens (1) FOCUS their interests and needs as they related to the Bible passage, (2) DISCOVER biblical truths and their implications for teen living, and (3) RESPOND in obedience to God and express that response in word or deed?

Do Yourself

Plan next week's lesson according to the *guided discovery learning* concept. Write down the real and felt needs of all your students as they relate to the central Bible truth to be taught. Determine the life-response aim in terms of what your students should feel and/or do in response to God's Word. Then plan FOCUS, DISCOVER, and RESPOND learning activities that will aid in accomplishing the life-response aim.

Prayer for Learning

Thank You, Lord, for the unfathomable treasures of Your Word. Thank You for the opportunity to discover Your will for our lives in its pages. For Your sake and theirs, help each teen in my class experience the joy of a changed heart and life through a personal discovery of Your will for his life. Amen.

5
"I'm Teaching a 'Mixed' Class"

One of the biggest challenges Frank and Helen face is teaching a class with an awkward mix of maturing and very immature young people, spiritually interested and spiritually dead teens, and older and younger high schoolers. Every year produces a new combination that comes with its own set of problems.

Like many others, the relatively small size of their church makes it hard to have more than one high school class. But they have found some ways to overcome the difficulty of a "mixed" class.

Because Frank and Helen usually teach the class together, the team-teaching approach is a helpful tool in reaching the different levels. By simply dividing the group into smaller groups according to age, sex, or interest, Frank and Helen can zero in more specifically on individual teens. For example, in a lesson on David and Bathsheba, Frank met with the guys and Helen met with the girls to discuss specific implications of the standards David and Bathsheba violated.

In another session when Helen was teaching the class by herself, she gave the teens a choice of joining one of two groups. Both groups prepared a report on God's perspective on the church. The first group studied Scriptures directly from the Bible, while the second group listened to a taped paraphrase and answered specific questions. The second group attracted the poor readers (common in many high school classes). Each group had a student leader, but Helen floated between the two groups to give guidance when needed.

Another way Frank and Helen overcame the difficulty of a "mixed" class is by concentrating on one-to-one relationships, especially with those teens who don't fit in too well with the rest of the group. This takes extra time, of course, but the Linquists find the effort pays rich benefits. For example, one year Glen was the only freshman boy in the class. The other boys were older and didn't include him in any of their outside activities. Frank began to spend time with Glen, and they became good friends. In the course of their friendship, they were able to discuss some of the biblical principles studied in class, and Frank helped Glen make his own personal applications. Because his problems were different from the older boys', Frank had difficulty making personal applications during class. But Glen responded enthusiastically when Frank helped him.

A third method Frank and Helen use is developing a *core group of committed teens* who are definitely interested in spiritual growth. The Linquists spend time discipling the young people individually and as a group during the week. Group members are committed to one another for prayer support and mutual encouragement toward spiritual growth. This nucleus of maturing Christian teens usually plays an important role in the class during the rest of the year. They spark class discussions and become effective group leaders when the class breaks up into small discussion groups.

Frank and Helen are always careful to keep this core group from becoming an exclusive clique. Group members are encouraged to practice discipleship by reaching out to other members of the class. Core members call or visit absentees and consciously help to draw out students who sit on the fringes. Juniors and seniors are encouraged to disciple a freshman or new member of the class. (Developing a core group is an important part of any church's total youth ministry. In larger churches, this group may be discipled by a different youth worker than the person responsible for a larger "mixed" Bible study group. But leaders of both groups should work together in supporting and encouraging the core group.)

A fourth way Frank and Helen face the challenge of a "mixed" class is through *prayer*. At first, this wasn't easy. A disciplined prayer life is a gap in most Christians' lives. But as they began to see the central role of the Holy Spirit in their teaching, the Linquists also began to realize that they needed to pray if they really wanted the Spirit to work.

They began by simply praying for every teen in the class by name, keeping specific needs in mind. They prayed for the Holy Spirit's work to be done in their lives. And, as time passed, God answered the Linquists' prayers. Students began to respond to God's Word and spiritual growth took place.

If you are teaching a high school group by yourself, find another adult who is interested in the teens to be a prayer partner with you. Ideally, you should meet on a regular basis to pray and plan with other adults who are involved with the teens in other areas of the church's total youth ministry.

Planting and Watering

Their experiences with the "mixed" class have taught Frank and Helen several important lessons about the teaching-learning process.

They no longer look at "teaching" as experts expounding

their knowledge to passive listeners. Instead, they see teaching as guiding learners through a process of discovery—a discovery of God's Word and its meaning for them today. This makes teaching an exciting experience.

The "mixed" class has also taught Frank and Helen the importance of personally responding to God in His Word. The more they study the Bible, the more they realize that God wants a response. Since each individual teen is unique, each must respond to God's commands and directions with his own mind, emotions, and will. Leading teens to this point of response is a continuous challenge.

Also, Frank and Helen have learned to watch for spiritual growth (described so simply in Galatians 5:22-23) in their teens' lives. Recognizing that their own spiritual growth doesn't always come easily makes them realistic and patient about what to expect in the lives of their teens.

Finally, Helen and Frank know exactly what Paul was talking about when he wrote to the Corinthians, "What, after all, is Apollos? And what is Paul? Only servants, through whom you came to believe—as the Lord has assigned to each His task, I planted the seed, Apollos watered it, but God made it grow. So neither he who plants nor he who waters is anything, but only God, who makes things grow" (1 Cor. 3:5-7).

Knowing that spiritual growth is a work of the Holy Spirit, the Linquists are patient and open to what He would do in the lives of the teenagers. When growth does not seem evident, they double-check their methods of planting and watering and keep on praying! When growth occurs, they know who to thank—the Master Teacher. And they're happy to be on His team!

Ask Yourself

What has my teaching experience taught me so far?

What do I look for in my students?
Where does prayer fit into my teaching?

Do Yourself

List all the teens in your class. Jot down a personal goal of yours for their lives. Then spend a few minutes praying for each of them.

Prayer for Effective Teaching

Lord, thank You for calling me to teach. Thank You for each one of the teens in my class. Empower me through Your Holy Spirit to teach effectively. For Your glory. Amen.

Resource Materials

Books about High School Youth
Hurley, Pat *The Magic Bubble* (An Analysis of Christian Youth). Wheaton, Ill.: Victor, 1978. Cat. No. 6-2181
A critical analysis of junior high and high school aged youth and the worldly philosophies that affect them.

Jessen, Dan and Harvey, George. *Understanding and Reaching Boys,* Wheaton, Ill.: Christian Service Brigade, 1972.
Some good sections on teenage boys.

Richards, Larry. *You, the Parent,* Chicago: Moody Press, 1974.
Practical help for parents. Deals with parent-teen relationships, communication through love, family unity, good discipline, parental authority, and family worship.

Books About High School Teaching
Gangel, Kenneth. *24 Ways to Improve Your Teaching,* Wheaton, Ill.: Victor, 1974. Cat. No. 6-2463
Tells how to use various methods of teaching effectively.

Mayes, Howard, and Long, James. *Can I Help It If They Don't Learn?* (Five Steps to Effective Learning). Wheaton, Ill.: Victor, 1977. Cat. No. 6-2755
A very practical book for anyone who teaches the Bible.

Reed, Bobbie and Johnson, Rex. *Bible Learning Activities,* Glendale, Calif.: Regal, 1974.
Another resource book of creative ideas.

Richards, Lawrence. *Creative Bible Teaching,* Chicago: Moody Press, 1970.
One of the best books ever written on teaching.
——— *You, the Teacher,* Chicago: Moody Press, 1972.
Written for all teachers. Practical and inspirational.

―――― *You and Youth,* Chicago: Moody Press, 1973.
A simplified version of *Creative Bible Teaching.*
Stoop, David. *Ways to Help Them Learn* (Youth), Glendale, Calif.: Regal, 1973.
An excellent textbook on teaching high school teens.
Towns, Elmer. *Successful Lesson Preparation,* Grand Rapids, Mich.: Baker, 1969.
Simple but basic.
Zuck, Roy. *Spiritual Power in Your Teaching,* Chicago: Moody Press, 1963.
Systematic treatment of the Holy Spirit in the teaching-learning process.

Books About Total Youth Ministry

Carroll, John and Ignatius, Keith. *Youth Ministry: Sunday, Monday, and Every Day,* Valley Forge, Pa.: Judson Press, 1972.
Another stimulating book that gives solid concepts for working with youth.
Hurley, Pat *Penetrating the Magic Bubble* (Developing a Successful Youth Ministry). Wheaton, Ill.: Victor, 1978. Cat. No. 6-2183
Gives practical help in developing a people-centered approach to a Bible-based youth ministry.
―――― *The Penetrators* (A Profile of Today's Successful Youth Worker). Wheaton, Ill.: Victor, 1978. Cat. No. 6-2184
Packed with practical suggestions and exercises that can help any youth worker become more effective reaching teens for Christ.
Richards, Larry. *Youth Ministry,* Grand Rapids, Mich.: Zondervan, 1972.
This book gives you the theory. Heavy reading. For the professional.
Richardson, Gary. *Where's It At?* (The Measure of Your Youth Ministry). Wheaton, Ill.: Victor, 1978. Cat. No. 6-2182
A practical tool to be used in evaluating and shaping a church's youth ministry. For lay and professional youth workers.

Newsletters and Cassette Tapes

Youthletter (formerly *Youth Today*), edited by James Reapsome. Twelve issues a year. Write the Evangelical Foundation, 1716 Spruce Street, Philadelphia, Pennsylvania 19103.
Success With Youth Report (formerly *Youth Report*), edited by Samuel and Edith Grafton. Twelve issues a year plus special reports.

Write Grafton Publications, 667 Madison Avenue, New York, New York 10021.

Youth Specialties Cassette Library. Write Youth Specialties, 861 Sixth Avenue, Suite 411, San Diego, California 92101